Watered
a daily journal of intention

Watered: a daily journal of intention

Printed in the United States of America

Kindle Direct Publishing

Cover Art: Purely Drea | www.purelydrea.com

A note from the author:

This journal was created to be used on its own or in supplementation with "Rooted: fifty-two weeks of intention" - the guided journal. The simple, repetitive nature of this book's format is meant to help you stay accountable to your goals, feelings, and intentions every day.

I have prayed over this book, over you, and over your growth from start to finish. May you seek and find the peace that surpasses all understanding as you dive deeper into living intentionally.

always love,
ka'ala

Watered: a daily journal of intention

Watered
a daily journal of intention
by ka'ala

___ / ___ / ___

Today's Intention:

_____

_____

Affirmation:_____

Major Tasks/Goals:

[ ] _____   [ ] _____

[ ] _____   [ ] _____

[ ] _____   [ ] _____

Today I am feeling…

_____

_____

_____

take a moment to release any fear, doubt, or negativity…

Three things I intend to do for myself:
(If reflecting, three things I did for myself)

1._____

2._____

3._____

How will I serve others?
(If reflecting, how did I serve others?)

_____

_____

_____

_____

Three things I am grateful for:

1. _____

2. _____

3. _____

talk about anything…

_____

_____

_____

_____

_____

_____

___ / ___ / ___

Today's Intention:

_____

_____

Affirmation:_____

Major Tasks/Goals:

[ ] _____   [ ] _____

[ ] _____   [ ] _____

[ ] _____   [ ] _____

Today I am feeling…

_____

_____

_____

take a moment to release any fear, doubt, or negativity…

Three things I intend to do for myself:
(If reflecting, three things I did for myself)

1._____

2._____

3._____

How will I serve others?
(If reflecting, how did I serve others?)

_____

_____

_____

_____

Three things I am grateful for:

1. _____

2. _____

3. _____

talk about anything…

_____

_____

_____

_____

_____

_____

___/___/___

Today's Intention:

_____

_____

Affirmation:_____

Major Tasks/Goals:

[.] _____   [ ] _____

[ ] _____   [ ] _____

[ ] _____   [ ] _____

Today I am feeling...

_____

_____

_____

take a moment to release any fear, doubt, or negativity...

Three things I intend to do for myself:
(If reflecting, three things I did for myself)

1._____

2._____

3._____

How will I serve others?
(If reflecting, how did I serve others?)

_____

_____

_____

_____

Three things I am grateful for:

1. _____

2. _____

3. _____

talk about anything…

_____

_____

_____

_____

_____

_____

___/___/___

Today's Intention:

_____

_____

Affirmation:_____

Major Tasks/Goals:

[ ] _____ [ ] _____

[ ] _____ [ ] _____

[ ] _____ [ ] _____

Today I am feeling…

_____

_____

_____

take a moment to release any fear, doubt, or negativity…

Three things I intend to do for myself:
(If reflecting, three things I did for myself)

1._____

2._____

3._____

Watered: a daily journal of intention

How will I serve others?
(If reflecting, how did I serve others?)

_____

_____

_____

_____

Three things I am grateful for:

1. _____

2. _____

3. _____

talk about anything…

_____

_____

_____

_____

_____

_____

_____

___/___/___

Today's Intention:

_____

_____

Affirmation:_____

Major Tasks/Goals:

[ ] _____   [ ] _____

[ ] _____   [ ] _____

[ ] _____   [ ] _____

Today I am feeling...

_____

_____

_____

take a moment to release any fear, doubt, or negativity...

Three things I intend to do for myself:
(If reflecting, three things I did for myself)

1._____

2._____

3._____

How will I serve others?
(If reflecting, how did I serve others?)

_____

_____

_____

_____

Three things I am grateful for:

1. _____

2. _____

3. _____

talk about anything...

_____

_____

_____

_____

_____

_____

Watered: a daily journal of intention

___/___/___

Today's Intention:

_____

_____

Affirmation:_____

Major Tasks/Goals:

[ ] _____   [ ] _____

[ ] _____   [ ] _____

[ ] _____   [ ] _____

Today I am feeling…

_____

_____

_____

take a moment to release any fear, doubt, or negativity…

Three things I intend to do for myself:
(If reflecting, three things I did for myself)

1._____

2._____

3._____

How will I serve others?
(If reflecting, how did I serve others?)

_____

_____

_____

_____

Three things I am grateful for:

1. _____

2. _____

3. _____

talk about anything…

_____

_____

_____

_____

_____

_____

_____ / _____ / _____

Today's Intention:

_____

_____

Affirmation:_____

Major Tasks/Goals:

[ ] _____ [ ] _____

[ ] _____ [ ] _____

[ ] _____ [ ] _____

Today I am feeling...

_____

_____

_____

take a moment to release any fear, doubt, or negativity...

Three things I intend to do for myself:
(If reflecting, three things I did for myself)

1._____

2._____

3._____

How will I serve others?
(If reflecting, how did I serve others?)

_____

_____

_____

_____

Three things I am grateful for:

1. _____

2. _____

3. _____

talk about anything…

_____

_____

_____

_____

_____

_____

___/ ___/ ___

Today's Intention:

_____

_____

Affirmation:_____

Major Tasks/Goals:

[ ] _____   [ ] _____

[ ] _____   [ ] _____

[ ] _____   [ ] _____

Today I am feeling…

_____

_____

_____

take a moment to release any fear, doubt, or negativity…

Three things I intend to do for myself:
(If reflecting, three things I did for myself)

1._____

2._____

3._____

How will I serve others?
(If reflecting, how did I serve others?)

_____

_____

_____

_____

Three things I am grateful for:

1. _____

2. _____

3. _____

talk about anything…

_____

_____

_____

_____

_____

_____

___/ ___/ ___

Today's Intention:

_____

_____

Affirmation:_____ _____

Major Tasks/Goals:

[ ] _____   [ ] _____

[ ] _____   [ ] _____

[ ] _____   [ ] _____

Today I am feeling…

_____

_____

_____

take a moment to release any fear, doubt, or negativity…

Three things I intend to do for myself:
(If reflecting, three things I did for myself)

1._____

2._____

3._____

How will I serve others?
(If reflecting, how did I serve others?)

_____

_____

_____

_____

Three things I am grateful for:

1. _____

2. _____

3. _____

talk about anything…

_____

_____

_____

_____

_____

_____

_____

___/ ___/ ___

Today's Intention:

_____

_____

Affirmation:_____

Major Tasks/Goals:

[ ] _____   [ ] _____

[ ] _____   [ ] _____

[ ] _____   [ ] _____

Today I am feeling...

_____

_____

_____

take a moment to release any fear, doubt, or negativity...

Three things I intend to do for myself:
(If reflecting, three things I did for myself)

1._____

2._____

3._____

How will I serve others?
(If reflecting, how did I serve others?)

_____

_____

_____

_____

Three things I am grateful for:

1. _____

2. _____

3. _____

talk about anything…

_____

_____

_____

_____

_____

_____

___/ ___/ ___

Today's Intention:

_____

_____

Affirmation:_____

Major Tasks/Goals:

[ ] _____   [ ] _____

[ ] _____   [ ] _____

[ ] _____   [ ] _____

Today I am feeling…

_____

_____

_____

take a moment to release any fear, doubt, or negativity…

Three things I intend to do for myself:
(If reflecting, three things I did for myself)

1._____

2._____

3._____

How will I serve others?
(If reflecting, how did I serve others?)

_____

_____

_____

_____

Three things I am grateful for:

1. _____

2. _____

3. _____

talk about anything...

_____

_____

_____

_____

_____

_____

_____

___ / ___ / ___

Today's Intention:

_____

_____

Affirmation:_____

Major Tasks/Goals:

[ ] _____   [ ] _____

[ ] _____   [ ] _____

[ ] _____   [ ] _____

Today I am feeling…

_____

_____

_____

take a moment to release any fear, doubt, or negativity…

Three things I intend to do for myself:
(If reflecting, three things I did for myself)

1._____

2._____

3._____

How will I serve others?
(If reflecting, how did I serve others?)

_____

_____

_____

_____

Three things I am grateful for:

1. _____

2. _____

3. _____

talk about anything…

_____

_____

_____

_____

_____

_____

___/ ___/ ___

Today's Intention:

_____

_____

Affirmation:_____

Major Tasks/Goals:

[ ] _____   [ ] _____

[ ] _____   [ ] _____

[ ] _____   [ ] _____

Today I am feeling…

_____

_____

_____

take a moment to release any fear, doubt, or negativity…

Three things I intend to do for myself:
(If reflecting, three things I did for myself)

1._____

2._____

3._____

How will I serve others?
(If reflecting, how did I serve others?)

_____

_____

_____

_____

Three things I am grateful for:

1. _____

2. _____

3. _____

talk about anything…

_____

_____

_____

_____

_____

_____

___/ ___/ ___

Today's Intention:

_____

_____

Affirmation:_____

Major Tasks/Goals:

[ ] _____   [ ] _____

[ ] _____   [ ] _____

[ ] _____   [ ] _____

Today I am feeling…

_____

_____

_____

take a moment to release any fear, doubt, or negativity…

Three things I intend to do for myself:
(If reflecting, three things I did for myself)

1._____

2._____

3._____

How will I serve others?
(If reflecting, how did I serve others?)

_____

_____

_____

_____

Three things I am grateful for:

1. _____

2. _____

3. _____

talk about anything…

_____

_____

_____

_____

_____

_____

_____

___/ ___/ ___

Today's Intention:

_____

_____

Affirmation:_____

Major Tasks/Goals:

[ ] _____   [ ] _____

[ ] _____   [ ] _____

[ ] _____   [ ] _____

Today I am feeling...

_____

_____

_____

take a moment to release any fear, doubt, or negativity...

Three things I intend to do for myself:
(If reflecting, three things I did for myself)

1._____

2._____

3._____

How will I serve others?
(If reflecting, how did I serve others?)

_____

_____

_____

_____

Three things I am grateful for:

1. _____

2. _____

3. _____

talk about anything…

_____

_____

_____

_____

_____

_____

___/ ___/ ___

Today's Intention:

_____

_____

Affirmation:_____

Major Tasks/Goals:

[ ] _____   [ ] _____

[ ] _____   [ ] _____

[ ] _____   [ ] _____

Today I am feeling...

_____

_____

_____

take a moment to release any fear, doubt, or negativity...

Three things I intend to do for myself:
(If reflecting, three things I did for myself)

1._____

2._____

3._____

How will I serve others?
(If reflecting, how did I serve others?)

_____

_____

_____

_____

Three things I am grateful for:

1. _____

2. _____

3. _____

talk about anything…

_____

_____

_____

_____

_____

_____

_____

___/___/___

Today's Intention:

_____

_____

Affirmation:_____

Major Tasks/Goals:

[ ] _____   [ ] _____

[ ] _____   [ ] _____

[ ] _____   [ ] _____

Today I am feeling…

_____

_____

_____

take a moment to release any fear, doubt, or negativity…

Three things I intend to do for myself:
(If reflecting, three things I did for myself)

1._____

2._____

3._____

How will I serve others?
(If reflecting, how did I serve others?)

_____

_____

_____

_____

Three things I am grateful for:

1. _____

2. _____

3. _____

talk about anything...

_____

_____

_____

_____

_____

_____

_____

___/ ___/ ___

Today's Intention:

_____

_____

Affirmation:_____

Major Tasks/Goals:

[ ] _____   [ ] _____

[ ] _____   [ ] _____

[ ] _____   [ ] _____

Today I am feeling...

_____

_____

_____

take a moment to release any fear, doubt, or negativity...

Three things I intend to do for myself:
(If reflecting, three things I did for myself)

1._____

2._____

3._____

How will I serve others?
(If reflecting, how did I serve others?)

_____

_____

_____

_____

Three things I am grateful for:

1. _____

2. _____

3. _____

talk about anything...

_____

_____

_____

_____

_____

_____

_____

___ / ___ / ___

Today's Intention:

_____

_____

Affirmation:_____

Major Tasks/Goals:

[ ] _____   [ ] _____

[ ] _____   [ ] _____

[ ] _____   [ ] _____

Today I am feeling…

_____

_____

_____

take a moment to release any fear, doubt, or negativity…

Three things I intend to do for myself:
(If reflecting, three things I did for myself)

1._____

2._____

3._____

How will I serve others?
(If reflecting, how did I serve others?)

_____

_____

_____

_____

Three things I am grateful for:

1. _____

2. _____

3. _____

talk about anything...

_____

_____

_____

_____

_____

_____

_____

___ / ___ / ___

Today's Intention:

_____

_____

Affirmation:_____

Major Tasks/Goals:

[ ] _____   [ ] _____

[ ] _____   [ ] _____

[ ] _____   [ ] _____

Today I am feeling...

_____

_____

_____

take a moment to release any fear, doubt, or negativity...

Three things I intend to do for myself:
(If reflecting, three things I did for myself)

1._____

2._____

3._____

How will I serve others?
(If reflecting, how did I serve others?)

_____

_____

_____

_____

Three things I am grateful for:

1. _____

2. _____

3. _____

talk about anything...

_____

_____

_____

_____

_____

_____

_____

___ / ___ / ___

Today's Intention:

_____

_____

Affirmation:_____

Major Tasks/Goals:

[ ] _____   [ ] _____

[ ] _____   [ ] _____

[ ] _____   [ ] _____

Today I am feeling…

_____

_____

_____

take a moment to release any fear, doubt, or negativity…

Three things I intend to do for myself:
(If reflecting, three things I did for myself)

1._____

2._____

3._____

How will I serve others?
(If reflecting, how did I serve others?)

_____

_____

_____

_____

Three things I am grateful for:

1. _____

2. _____

3. _____

talk about anything…

_____

_____

_____

_____

_____

_____

_____

Watered: a daily journal of intention

___ / ___ / ___

Today's Intention:

_____

_____

Affirmation:_____

Major Tasks/Goals:

[ ] _____   [ ] _____

[ ] _____   [ ] _____

[ ] _____   [ ] _____

Today I am feeling…

_____

_____

_____

take a moment to release any fear, doubt, or negativity…

Three things I intend to do for myself:
(If reflecting, three things I did for myself)

1._____

2._____

3._____

How will I serve others?
(If reflecting, how did I serve others?)

_____

_____

_____

_____

Three things I am grateful for:

1. _____

2. _____

3. _____

talk about anything...

_____

_____

_____

_____

_____

_____

_____

___/ ___/ ___

Today's Intention:

_____

_____

Affirmation:_____

Major Tasks/Goals:

[ ] _____   [ ] _____

[ ] _____   [ ] _____

[ ] _____   [ ] _____

Today I am feeling…

_____

_____

_____

take a moment to release any fear, doubt, or negativity…

Three things I intend to do for myself:
(If reflecting, three things I did for myself)

1._____

2._____

3._____

How will I serve others?
(If reflecting, how did I serve others?)

_____

_____

_____

_____

Three things I am grateful for:

1. _____

2. _____

3. _____

talk about anything…

_____

_____

_____

_____

_____

_____

_____

___/___/___

Today's Intention:

_____

_____

Affirmation:_____

Major Tasks/Goals:

[ ] _____   [ ] _____

[ ] _____   [ ] _____

[ ] _____   [ ] _____

Today I am feeling…

_____

_____

_____

take a moment to release any fear, doubt, or negativity…

Three things I intend to do for myself:
(If reflecting, three things I did for myself)

1._____

2._____

3._____

How will I serve others?
(If reflecting, how did I serve others?)

_____

_____

_____

_____

Three things I am grateful for:

1. _____

2. _____

3. _____

talk about anything...

_____

_____

_____

_____

_____

_____

_____

____/____/____

Today's Intention:

_____

_____

Affirmation:_____

Major Tasks/Goals:

[ ] _____   [ ] _____

[ ] _____   [ ] _____

[ ] _____   [ ] _____

Today I am feeling...

_____

_____

_____

take a moment to release any fear, doubt, or negativity...

Three things I intend to do for myself:
(If reflecting, three things I did for myself)

1._____

2._____

3._____

How will I serve others?
(If reflecting, how did I serve others?)

_____

_____

_____

_____

Three things I am grateful for:

1. _____

2. _____

3. _____

talk about anything...

_____

_____

_____

_____

_____

_____

_____

___ / ___ / ___

Today's Intention:

_____

_____

Affirmation:_____

Major Tasks/Goals:

[ ] _____   [ ] _____

[ ] _____   [ ] _____

[ ] _____   [ ] _____

Today I am feeling…

_____

_____

_____

take a moment to release any fear, doubt, or negativity…

Three things I intend to do for myself:
(If reflecting, three things I did for myself)

1._____

2._____

3._____

How will I serve others?
(If reflecting, how did I serve others?)

_____

_____

_____

_____

Three things I am grateful for:

1. _____

2. _____

3. _____

talk about anything...

_____

_____

_____

_____

_____

_____

_____

___ / ___ / ___

Today's Intention:

_____

_____

Affirmation:_____

Major Tasks/Goals:

[ ] _____   [ ] _____

[ ] _____   [ ] _____

[ ] _____   [ ] _____

Today I am feeling…

_____

_____

_____

take a moment to release any fear, doubt, or negativity…

Three things I intend to do for myself:
(If reflecting, three things I did for myself)

1._____

2._____

3._____

How will I serve others?
(If reflecting, how did I serve others?)

_____

_____

_____

_____

Three things I am grateful for:

1. _____

2. _____

3. _____

talk about anything...

_____

_____

_____

_____

_____

_____

_____

___/___/___

Today's Intention:

_____

_____

Affirmation:_____

Major Tasks/Goals:

[ ] _____   [ ] _____

[ ] _____   [ ] _____

[ ] _____   [ ] _____

Today I am feeling…

_____

_____

_____

take a moment to release any fear, doubt, or negativity…

Three things I intend to do for myself:
(If reflecting, three things I did for myself)

1._____

2._____

3._____

How will I serve others?
(If reflecting, how did I serve others?)

_____

_____

_____

_____

Three things I am grateful for:

1. _____

2. _____

3. _____

talk about anything...

_____

_____

_____

_____

_____

_____

_____

___/ ___/ ___

Today's Intention:

_____

_____

Affirmation:_____

Major Tasks/Goals:

[ ] _____   [ ] _____

[ ] _____   [ ] _____

[ ] _____   [ ] _____

Today I am feeling...

_____

_____

_____

take a moment to release any fear, doubt, or negativity...

Three things I intend to do for myself:
(If reflecting, three things I did for myself)

1._____

2._____

3._____

How will I serve others?
(If reflecting, how did I serve others?)

_____

_____

_____

_____

Three things I am grateful for:

1. _____

2. _____

3. _____

talk about anything...

_____

_____

_____

_____

_____

_____

_____

___/___/___

Today's Intention:

_____

_____

Affirmation:_____

Major Tasks/Goals:

[ ] _____   [ ] _____

[ ] _____   [ ] _____

[ ] _____   [ ] _____

Today I am feeling…

_____

_____

_____

take a moment to release any fear, doubt, or negativity…

Three things I intend to do for myself:
(If reflecting, three things I did for myself)

1._____

2._____

3._____

How will I serve others?
(If reflecting, how did I serve others?)

_____

_____

_____

_____

Three things I am grateful for:

1. _____

2. _____

3. _____

talk about anything...

_____

_____

_____

_____

_____

_____

_____

MONTHLY CHECK-IN

This month was .... ☺ ☹

Did I meet my goals? .... YES! Still at it!

I feel _____ about next month.

I will celebrate my accomplishments by:

_____

_____

My favorite affirmation from this month is:

_____

_____

A doodle of this month's progress (it does not need to be linear)

notes to self…

_____

_____

_____

_____

_____

_____

_____

_____

_____

_____

_____

_____

_____

_____

_____

_____

_____

_____

___ / ___ / ___

Today's Intention:

_____

_____

Affirmation:_____

Major Tasks/Goals:

[ ] _____   [ ] _____

[ ] _____   [ ] _____

[ ] _____   [ ] _____

Today I am feeling...

_____

_____

_____

take a moment to release any fear, doubt, or negativity...

Three things I intend to do for myself:
(If reflecting, three things I did for myself)

1._____

2._____

3._____

How will I serve others?
(If reflecting, how did I serve others?)

_____

_____

_____

_____

Three things I am grateful for:

1. _____

2. _____

3. _____

talk about anything...

_____

_____

_____

_____

_____

_____

_____

___/___/___

Today's Intention:

_____

_____

Affirmation:_____

Major Tasks/Goals:

[ ] _____   [ ] _____

[ ] _____   [ ] _____

[ ] _____   [ ] _____

Today I am feeling...

_____

_____

_____

take a moment to release any fear, doubt, or negativity...

Three things I intend to do for myself:
(If reflecting, three things I did for myself)

1._____

2._____

3._____

How will I serve others?
(If reflecting, how did I serve others?)

_____

_____

_____

_____

Three things I am grateful for:

1. _____

2. _____

3. _____

talk about anything…

_____

_____

_____

_____

_____

_____

_____

___/___/___

Today's Intention:

_____

_____

Affirmation:_____

Major Tasks/Goals:

[ ] _____   [ ] _____

[ ] _____   [ ] _____

[ ] _____   [ ] _____

Today I am feeling…

_____

_____

_____

take a moment to release any fear, doubt, or negativity…

Three things I intend to do for myself:
(If reflecting, three things I did for myself)

1._____

2._____

3._____

How will I serve others?
(If reflecting, how did I serve others?)

_____

_____

_____

_____

Three things I am grateful for:

1. _____

2. _____

3. _____

talk about anything...

_____

_____

_____

_____

_____

_____

_____

___/___/___

Today's Intention:

_____

_____

Affirmation:_____

Major Tasks/Goals:

[ ] _____   [ ] _____

[ ] _____   [ ] _____

[ ] _____   [ ] _____

Today I am feeling…

_____

_____

_____

take a moment to release any fear, doubt, or negativity…

Three things I intend to do for myself:
(If reflecting, three things I did for myself)

1._____

2._____

3._____

How will I serve others?
(If reflecting, how did I serve others?)

_____

_____

_____

_____

Three things I am grateful for:

1. _____

2. _____

3. _____

talk about anything...

_____

_____

_____

_____

_____

_____

_____

___ / ___ / ___

Today's Intention:

_____

_____

Affirmation:_____

Major Tasks/Goals:

[ ] _____   [ ] _____

[ ] _____   [ ] _____

[ ] _____   [ ] _____

Today I am feeling...

_____

_____

_____

take a moment to release any fear, doubt, or negativity...

Three things I intend to do for myself:
(If reflecting, three things I did for myself)

1._____

2._____

3._____

How will I serve others?
(If reflecting, how did I serve others?)

_____

_____

_____

_____

Three things I am grateful for:

1. _____

2. _____

3. _____

talk about anything…

_____

_____

_____

_____

_____

_____

_____

___/___/___

Today's Intention:

_____

_____

Affirmation:_____

Major Tasks/Goals:

[ ] _____   [ ] _____

[ ] _____   [ ] _____

[ ] _____   [ ] _____

Today I am feeling...

_____

_____

_____

take a moment to release any fear, doubt, or negativity...

Three things I intend to do for myself:
(If reflecting, three things I did for myself)

1._____

2._____

3._____

How will I serve others?
(If reflecting, how did I serve others?)

_____

_____

_____

_____

Three things I am grateful for:

1. _____

2. _____

3. _____

talk about anything…

_____

_____

_____

_____

_____

_____

_____

___/___/___

Today's Intention:

_____

_____

Affirmation:_____

Major Tasks/Goals:

[ ] _____   [ ] _____

[ ] _____   [ ] _____

[ ] _____   [ ] _____

Today I am feeling...

_____

_____

_____

take a moment to release any fear, doubt, or negativity...

Three things I intend to do for myself:
(If reflecting, three things I did for myself)

1._____

2._____

3._____

How will I serve others?
(If reflecting, how did I serve others?)

_____

_____

_____

_____

Three things I am grateful for:

1. _____

2. _____

3. _____

talk about anything...

_____

_____

_____

_____

_____

_____

___ / ___ / ___

Today's Intention:

_____

_____

Affirmation:_____

Major Tasks/Goals:

[ ] _____   [ ] _____

[ ] _____   [ ] _____

[ ] _____   [ ] _____

Today I am feeling…

_____

_____

_____

take a moment to release any fear, doubt, or negativity…

Three things I intend to do for myself:
(If reflecting, three things I did for myself)

1._____

2._____

3._____

How will I serve others?
(If reflecting, how did I serve others?)

_____

_____

_____

_____

Three things I am grateful for:

1. _____

2. _____

3. _____

talk about anything…

_____

_____

_____

_____

_____

_____

_____

___ / ___ / ___

Today's Intention:

_____

_____

Affirmation:_____

Major Tasks/Goals:

[ ] _____   [ ] _____

[ ] _____   [ ] _____

[ ] _____   [ ] _____

Today I am feeling...

_____

_____

_____

take a moment to release any fear, doubt, or negativity...

Three things I intend to do for myself:
(If reflecting, three things I did for myself)

1._____

2._____

3._____

How will I serve others?
(If reflecting, how did I serve others?)

_____

_____

_____

_____

Three things I am grateful for:

1. _____

2. _____

3. _____

talk about anything…

_____

_____

_____

_____

_____

_____

___/ ___/ ___

Today's Intention:

_____

_____

Affirmation:_____

Major Tasks/Goals:

[ ] _____   [ ] _____

[ ] _____   [ ] _____

[ ] _____   [ ] _____

Today I am feeling…

_____

_____

_____

take a moment to release any fear, doubt, or negativity…

Three things I intend to do for myself:
(If reflecting, three things I did for myself)

1._____

2._____

3._____

How will I serve others?
(If reflecting, how did I serve others?)

_____

_____

_____

_____

Three things I am grateful for:

1. _____

2. _____

3. _____

talk about anything...

_____

_____

_____

_____

_____

_____

___/___/___

Today's Intention:

_____

_____

Affirmation:_____

Major Tasks/Goals:

[ ] _____   [ ] _____

[ ] _____   [ ] _____

[ ] _____   [ ] _____

Today I am feeling…

_____

_____

_____

take a moment to release any fear, doubt, or negativity…

Three things I intend to do for myself:
(If reflecting, three things I did for myself)

1._____

2._____

3._____

How will I serve others?
(If reflecting, how did I serve others?)

_____

_____

_____

_____

Three things I am grateful for:

1. _____

2. _____

3. _____

talk about anything...

_____

_____

_____

_____

_____

_____

_____

___ / ___ / ___

Today's Intention:

_____

_____

Affirmation:_____

Major Tasks/Goals:

[ ] _____   [ ] _____

[ ] _____   [ ] _____

[ ] _____   [ ] _____

Today I am feeling…

_____

_____

_____

take a moment to release any fear, doubt, or negativity…

Three things I intend to do for myself:
(If reflecting, three things I did for myself)

1._____

2._____

3._____

Watered: a daily journal of intention

How will I serve others?
(If reflecting, how did I serve others?)

_____

_____

_____

_____

Three things I am grateful for:

1. _____

2. _____

3. _____

talk about anything...

_____

_____

_____

_____

_____

_____

_____

___/___/___

Today's Intention:

_____

_____

Affirmation:_____

Major Tasks/Goals:

[ ] _____   [ ] _____

[ ] _____   [ ] _____

[ ] _____   [ ] _____

Today I am feeling...

_____

_____

_____

take a moment to release any fear, doubt, or negativity...

Three things I intend to do for myself:
(If reflecting, three things I did for myself)

1._____

2._____

3._____

How will I serve others?
(If reflecting, how did I serve others?)

_____

_____

_____

_____

Three things I am grateful for:

1. _____

2. _____

3. _____

talk about anything...

_____

_____

_____

_____

_____

_____

___/ ___/ ___

Today's Intention:

_____

_____

Affirmation:_____

Major Tasks/Goals:

[ ] _____   [ ] _____

[ ] _____   [ ] _____

[ ] _____   [ ] _____

Today I am feeling…

_____

_____

_____

take a moment to release any fear, doubt, or negativity…

Three things I intend to do for myself:
(If reflecting, three things I did for myself)

1._____

2._____

3._____

How will I serve others?
(If reflecting, how did I serve others?)

_____

_____

_____

_____

Three things I am grateful for:

1. _____

2. _____

3. _____

talk about anything…

_____

_____

_____

_____

_____

_____

_____

___ / ___ / ___

Today's Intention:

_____

_____

Affirmation:_____

Major Tasks/Goals:

[ ] _____   [ ] _____

[ ] _____   [ ] _____

[ ] _____   [ ] _____

Today I am feeling...

_____

_____

_____

take a moment to release any fear, doubt, or negativity...

Three things I intend to do for myself:
(If reflecting, three things I did for myself)

1._____

2._____

3._____

How will I serve others?
(If reflecting, how did I serve others?)

_____

_____

_____

_____

Three things I am grateful for:

1. _____

2. _____

3. _____

talk about anything…

_____

_____

_____

_____

_____

_____

_____

___ / ___ / ___

Today's Intention:

_____

_____

Affirmation:_____

Major Tasks/Goals:

[ ] _____   [ ] _____

[ ] _____   [ ] _____

[ ] _____   [ ] _____

Today I am feeling…

_____

_____

_____

take a moment to release any fear, doubt, or negativity…

Three things I intend to do for myself:
(If reflecting, three things I did for myself)

1._____

2._____

3._____

How will I serve others?
(If reflecting, how did I serve others?)

_____

_____

_____

_____

Three things I am grateful for:

1. _____

2. _____

3. _____

talk about anything...

_____

_____

_____

_____

_____

_____

_____

___ / ___ / ___

Today's Intention:

_____

_____

Affirmation:_____

Major Tasks/Goals:

[ ] _____   [ ] _____

[ ] _____   [ ] _____

[ ] _____   [ ] _____

Today I am feeling...

_____

_____

_____

take a moment to release any fear, doubt, or negativity...

Three things I intend to do for myself:
(If reflecting, three things I did for myself)

1._____

2._____

3._____

How will I serve others?
(If reflecting, how did I serve others?)

_____

_____

_____

_____

Three things I am grateful for:

1. _____

2. _____

3. _____

talk about anything...

_____

_____

_____

_____

_____

_____

_____

___/ ___/ ___

Today's Intention:

_____

_____

Affirmation:_____

Major Tasks/Goals:

[ ] _____   [ ] _____

[ ] _____   [ ] _____

[ ] _____   [ ] _____

Today I am feeling…

_____

_____

_____

take a moment to release any fear, doubt, or negativity…

Three things I intend to do for myself:
(If reflecting, three things I did for myself)

1._____

2._____

3._____

How will I serve others?
(If reflecting, how did I serve others?)

_____

_____

_____

_____

Three things I am grateful for:

1. _____

2. _____

3. _____

talk about anything...

_____

_____

_____

_____

_____

_____

_____

___/ ___/ ___

Today's Intention:

_____

_____

Affirmation:_____

Major Tasks/Goals:

[ ] _____   [ ] _____

[ ] _____   [ ] _____

[ ] _____   [ ] _____

Today I am feeling…

_____

_____

_____

take a moment to release any fear, doubt, or negativity…

Three things I intend to do for myself:
(If reflecting, three things I did for myself)

1._____

2._____

3._____

How will I serve others?
(If reflecting, how did I serve others?)

_____

_____

_____

_____

Three things I am grateful for:

1. _____

2. _____

3. _____

talk about anything...

_____

_____

_____

_____

_____

_____

_____

___/___/___

Today's Intention:

_____

_____

Affirmation:_____

Major Tasks/Goals:

[ ] _____   [ ] _____

[ ] _____   [ ] _____

[ ] _____   [ ] _____

Today I am feeling...

_____

_____

_____

take a moment to release any fear, doubt, or negativity...

Three things I intend to do for myself:
(If reflecting, three things I did for myself)

1._____

2._____

3._____

How will I serve others?
(If reflecting, how did I serve others?)

_____

_____

_____

_____

Three things I am grateful for:

1. _____

2. _____

3. _____

talk about anything...

_____

_____

_____

_____

_____

_____

_____

___ / ___ / ___

Today's Intention:

_____

_____

Affirmation:_____

Major Tasks/Goals:

[ ] _____   [ ] _____

[ ] _____   [ ] _____

[ ] _____   [ ] _____

Today I am feeling...

_____

_____

_____

take a moment to release any fear, doubt, or negativity...

Three things I intend to do for myself:
(If reflecting, three things I did for myself)

1._____

2._____

3._____

How will I serve others?
(If reflecting, how did I serve others?)

_____

_____

_____

_____

Three things I am grateful for:

1. _____

2. _____

3. _____

talk about anything...

_____

_____

_____

_____

_____

_____

___/___/___

Today's Intention:

_____

_____

Affirmation:_____

Major Tasks/Goals:

[ ] _____   [ ] _____

[ ] _____   [ ] _____

[ ] _____   [ ] _____

Today I am feeling…

_____

_____

_____

take a moment to release any fear, doubt, or negativity…

Three things I intend to do for myself:
(If reflecting, three things I did for myself)

1._____

2._____

3._____

How will I serve others?
(If reflecting, how did I serve others?)

_____

_____

_____

_____

Three things I am grateful for:

1. _____

2. _____

3. _____

talk about anything...

_____

_____

_____

_____

_____

_____

_____

___/ ___/ ___

Today's Intention:

_____

_____

Affirmation:_____

Major Tasks/Goals:

[ ] _____   [ ] _____

[ ] _____   [ ] _____

[ ] _____   [ ] _____

Today I am feeling...

_____

_____

_____

take a moment to release any fear, doubt, or negativity...

Three things I intend to do for myself:
(If reflecting, three things I did for myself)

1._____

2._____

3._____

How will I serve others?
(If reflecting, how did I serve others?)

_____

_____

_____

_____

Three things I am grateful for:

1. _____

2. _____

3. _____

talk about anything...

_____

_____

_____

_____

_____

_____

_____

Watered: a daily journal of intention

___/___/___

Today's Intention:

_____

_____

Affirmation:_____

Major Tasks/Goals:

[ ] _____   [ ] _____

[ ] _____   [ ] _____

[ ] _____   [ ] _____

Today I am feeling...

_____

_____

_____

take a moment to release any fear, doubt, or negativity...

Three things I intend to do for myself:
(If reflecting, three things I did for myself)

1._____

2._____

3._____

How will I serve others?
(If reflecting, how did I serve others?)

_____

_____

_____

_____

Three things I am grateful for:

1. _____

2. _____

3. _____

talk about anything…

_____

_____

_____

_____

_____

_____

_____

___/ ___/ ___

Today's Intention:

_____

_____

Affirmation:_____

Major Tasks/Goals:

[ ] _____   [ ] _____

[ ] _____   [ ] _____

[ ] _____   [ ] _____

Today I am feeling…

_____

_____

_____

take a moment to release any fear, doubt, or negativity…

Three things I intend to do for myself:
(If reflecting, three things I did for myself)

1._____

2._____

3._____

How will I serve others?
(If reflecting, how did I serve others?)

_____

_____

_____

_____

Three things I am grateful for:

1. _____

2. _____

3. _____

talk about anything…

_____

_____

_____

_____

_____

_____

___/___/___

Today's Intention:

_____

_____

Affirmation:_____

Major Tasks/Goals:

[ ] _____   [ ] _____

[ ] _____   [ ] _____

[ ] _____   [ ] _____

Today I am feeling...

_____

_____

_____

take a moment to release any fear, doubt, or negativity...

Three things I intend to do for myself:
(If reflecting, three things I did for myself)

1._____

2._____

3._____

How will I serve others?
(If reflecting, how did I serve others?)

_____

_____

_____

_____

Three things I am grateful for:

1. _____

2. _____

3. _____

talk about anything…

_____

_____

_____

_____

_____

_____

_____

___/___/___

Today's Intention:

_____

_____

Affirmation:_____

Major Tasks/Goals:

[ ] _____   [ ] _____

[ ] _____   [ ] _____

[ ] _____   [ ] _____

Today I am feeling…

_____

_____

_____

take a moment to release any fear, doubt, or negativity…

Three things I intend to do for myself:
(If reflecting, three things I did for myself)

1._____

2._____

3._____

How will I serve others?
(If reflecting, how did I serve others?)

_____

_____

_____

_____

Three things I am grateful for:

1. _____

2. _____

3. _____

talk about anything…

_____

_____

_____

_____

_____

_____

_____

___/ ___/ ___

Today's Intention:

_____

_____

Affirmation:_____

Major Tasks/Goals:

[ ] _____   [ ] _____

[ ] _____   [ ] _____

[ ] _____   [ ] _____

Today I am feeling…

_____

_____

_____

take a moment to release any fear, doubt, or negativity…

Three things I intend to do for myself:
(If reflecting, three things I did for myself)

1._____

2._____

3._____

How will I serve others?
(If reflecting, how did I serve others?)

_____

_____

_____

_____

Three things I am grateful for:

1. _____

2. _____

3. _____

talk about anything...

_____

_____

_____

_____

_____

_____

___/___/___

Today's Intention:

_____

_____

Affirmation:_____

Major Tasks/Goals:

[ ] _____   [ ] _____

[ ] _____   [ ] _____

[ ] _____   [ ] _____

Today I am feeling...

_____

_____

_____

take a moment to release any fear, doubt, or negativity...

Three things I intend to do for myself:
(If reflecting, three things I did for myself)

1._____

2._____

3._____

How will I serve others?
(If reflecting, how did I serve others?)

_____

_____

_____

_____

Three things I am grateful for:

1. _____

2. _____

3. _____

talk about anything…

_____

_____

_____

_____

_____

_____

Watered: a daily journal of intention

___/ ___/ ___

Today's Intention:

_____

_____

Affirmation:_____

Major Tasks/Goals:

[ ] _____   [ ] _____

[ ] _____   [ ] _____

[ ] _____   [ ] _____

Today I am feeling...

_____

_____

_____

take a moment to release any fear, doubt, or negativity...

Three things I intend to do for myself:
(If reflecting, three things I did for myself)

1._____

2._____

3._____

How will I serve others?
(If reflecting, how did I serve others?)

_____

_____

_____

_____

Three things I am grateful for:

1. _____

2. _____

3. _____

talk about anything…

_____

_____

_____

_____

_____

_____

_____

MONTHLY CHECK-IN

This month was ……………………………….. ☺   ☹

Did I meet my goals? ……………………… YES!   Still at it!

I feel _____ about next month.

I will celebrate my accomplishments by:

_____

_____

My favorite affirmation from this month is:

_____

_____

A doodle of this month's progress (it does not need to be linear)

notes to self...

_____

_____

_____

_____

_____

_____

_____

_____

_____

_____

_____

_____

_____

_____

_____

_____

_____

___/___/___

Today's Intention:

_____

_____

Affirmation:_____

Major Tasks/Goals:

[ ] _____   [ ] _____

[ ] _____   [ ] _____

[ ] _____   [ ] _____

Today I am feeling...

_____

_____

_____

take a moment to release any fear, doubt, or negativity...

Three things I intend to do for myself:
(If reflecting, three things I did for myself)

1._____

2._____

3._____

How will I serve others?
(If reflecting, how did I serve others?)

_____

_____

_____

_____

Three things I am grateful for:

1. _____

2. _____

3. _____

talk about anything...

_____

_____

_____

_____

_____

_____

_____

___/ ___/ ___

Today's Intention:

_____

_____

Affirmation:_____

Major Tasks/Goals:

[ ] _____   [ ] _____

[ ] _____   [ ] _____

[ ] _____   [ ] _____

Today I am feeling...

_____

_____

_____

take a moment to release any fear, doubt, or negativity...

Three things I intend to do for myself:
(If reflecting, three things I did for myself)

1._____

2._____

3._____

How will I serve others?
(If reflecting, how did I serve others?)

_____

_____

_____

_____

Three things I am grateful for:

1. _____

2. _____

3. _____

talk about anything...

_____

_____

_____

_____

_____

_____

_____

___ / ___ / ___

Today's Intention:

_____

_____

Affirmation:_____

Major Tasks/Goals:

[ ] _____   [ ] _____

[ ] _____   [ ] _____

[ ] _____   [ ] _____

Today I am feeling...

_____

_____

_____

take a moment to release any fear, doubt, or negativity...

Three things I intend to do for myself:
(If reflecting, three things I did for myself)

1._____

2._____

3._____

How will I serve others?
(If reflecting, how did I serve others?)

_____

_____

_____

_____

Three things I am grateful for:

1. _____

2. _____

3. _____

talk about anything...

_____

_____

_____

_____

_____

_____

_____

___/ ___/ ___

Today's Intention:

_____

_____

Affirmation:_____

Major Tasks/Goals:

[ ] _____   [ ] _____

[ ] _____   [ ] _____

[ ] _____   [ ] _____

Today I am feeling...

_____

_____

_____

take a moment to release any fear, doubt, or negativity...

Three things I intend to do for myself:
(If reflecting, three things I did for myself)

1._____

2._____

3._____

How will I serve others?
(If reflecting, how did I serve others?)

_____

_____

_____

_____

Three things I am grateful for:

1. _____

2. _____

3. _____

talk about anything…

_____

_____

_____

_____

_____

_____

_____

___/___/___

Today's Intention:

_____

_____

Affirmation:_____

Major Tasks/Goals:

[ ] _____   [ ] _____

[ ] _____   [ ] _____

[ ] _____   [ ] _____

Today I am feeling...

_____

_____

_____

take a moment to release any fear, doubt, or negativity...

Three things I intend to do for myself:
(If reflecting, three things I did for myself)

1._____

2._____

3._____

How will I serve others?
(If reflecting, how did I serve others?)

_____

_____

_____

_____

Three things I am grateful for:

1. _____

2. _____

3. _____

talk about anything…

_____

_____

_____

_____

_____

_____

_____

___ / ___ / ___

Today's Intention:

_____

_____

Affirmation:_____

Major Tasks/Goals:

[ ] _____   [ ] _____

[ ] _____   [ ] _____

[ ] _____   [ ] _____

Today I am feeling...

_____

_____

_____

take a moment to release any fear, doubt, or negativity...

Three things I intend to do for myself:
(If reflecting, three things I did for myself)

1._____

2._____

3._____

How will I serve others?
(If reflecting, how did I serve others?)

_____

_____

_____

_____

Three things I am grateful for:

1. _____

2. _____

3. _____

talk about anything...

_____

_____

_____

_____

_____

_____

_____

___/ ___/ ___

Today's Intention:

_____

_____

Affirmation:_____

Major Tasks/Goals:

[ ] _____   [ ] _____

[ ] _____   [ ] _____

[ ] _____   [ ] _____

Today I am feeling...

_____

_____

_____

take a moment to release any fear, doubt, or negativity...

Three things I intend to do for myself:
(If reflecting, three things I did for myself)

1._____

2._____

3._____

How will I serve others?
(If reflecting, how did I serve others?)

_____

_____

_____

_____

Three things I am grateful for:

1. _____

2. _____

3. _____

talk about anything…

_____

_____

_____

_____

_____

_____

___/ ___/ ___

Today's Intention:

_____

_____

Affirmation:_____

Major Tasks/Goals:

[ ] _____   [ ] _____

[ ] _____   [ ] _____

[ ] _____   [ ] _____

Today I am feeling...

_____

_____

_____

take a moment to release any fear, doubt, or negativity...

Three things I intend to do for myself:
(If reflecting, three things I did for myself)

1._____

2._____

3._____

How will I serve others?
(If reflecting, how did I serve others?)

_____

_____

_____

_____

Three things I am grateful for:

1. _____

2. _____

3. _____

talk about anything…

_____

_____

_____

_____

_____

_____

_____

___/___/___

Today's Intention:

_____

_____

Affirmation:_____

Major Tasks/Goals:

[ ] _____   [ ] _____

[ ] _____   [ ] _____

[ ] _____   [ ] _____

Today I am feeling...

_____

_____

_____

take a moment to release any fear, doubt, or negativity...

Three things I intend to do for myself:
(If reflecting, three things I did for myself)

1._____

2._____

3._____

How will I serve others?
(If reflecting, how did I serve others?)

_____

_____

_____

_____

Three things I am grateful for:

1. _____

2. _____

3. _____

talk about anything...

_____

_____

_____

_____

_____

_____

_____

Watered: a daily journal of intention

___/___/___

Today's Intention:

_____

_____

Affirmation:_____

Major Tasks/Goals:

[ ] _____   [ ] _____

[ ] _____   [ ] _____

[ ] _____   [ ] _____

Today I am feeling…

_____

_____

_____

take a moment to release any fear, doubt, or negativity…

Three things I intend to do for myself:
(If reflecting, three things I did for myself)

1._____

2._____

3._____

How will I serve others?
(If reflecting, how did I serve others?)

_____

_____

_____

_____

Three things I am grateful for:

1. _____

2. _____

3. _____

talk about anything...

_____

_____

_____

_____

_____

_____

_____

___/___/___

Today's Intention:

_____

_____

Affirmation:_____

Major Tasks/Goals:

[ ] _____   [ ] _____

[ ] _____   [ ] _____

[ ] _____   [ ] _____

Today I am feeling...

_____

_____

_____

take a moment to release any fear, doubt, or negativity...

Three things I intend to do for myself:
(If reflecting, three things I did for myself)

1._____

2._____

3._____

How will I serve others?
(If reflecting, how did I serve others?)

_____

_____

_____

_____

Three things I am grateful for:

1. _____

2. _____

3. _____

talk about anything...

_____

_____

_____

_____

_____

_____

_____

___/ ___/ ___

Today's Intention:

_____

_____

Affirmation:_____

Major Tasks/Goals:

[ ] _____   [ ] _____

[ ] _____   [ ] _____

[ ] _____   [ ] _____

Today I am feeling…

_____

_____

_____

take a moment to release any fear, doubt, or negativity…

Three things I intend to do for myself:
(If reflecting, three things I did for myself)

1._____

2._____

3._____

How will I serve others?
(If reflecting, how did I serve others?)

_____

_____

_____

_____

Three things I am grateful for:

1. _____

2. _____

3. _____

talk about anything…

_____

_____

_____

_____

_____

_____

_____

Watered: a daily journal of intention

___/___/___

Today's Intention:

_____

_____

Affirmation:_____

Major Tasks/Goals:

[ ] _____   [ ] _____

[ ] _____   [ ] _____

[ ] _____   [ ] _____

Today I am feeling...

_____

_____

_____

take a moment to release any fear, doubt, or negativity...

Three things I intend to do for myself:
(If reflecting, three things I did for myself)

1._____

2._____

3._____

How will I serve others?
(If reflecting, how did I serve others?)

_____

_____

_____

_____

Three things I am grateful for:

1. _____

2. _____

3. _____

talk about anything…

_____

_____

_____

_____

_____

_____

_____

___ / ___ / ___

Today's Intention:

_____

_____

Affirmation:_____

Major Tasks/Goals:

[ ] _____   [ ] _____

[ ] _____   [ ] _____

[ ] _____   [ ] _____

Today I am feeling…

_____

_____

_____

take a moment to release any fear, doubt, or negativity…

Three things I intend to do for myself:
(If reflecting, three things I did for myself)

1._____

2._____

3._____

How will I serve others?
(If reflecting, how did I serve others?)

_____

_____

_____

_____

Three things I am grateful for:

1. _____

2. _____

3. _____

talk about anything...

_____

_____

_____

_____

_____

_____

_____

___/ ___/ ___

Today's Intention:

_____

_____

Affirmation:_____

Major Tasks/Goals:

[ ] _____   [ ] _____

[ ] _____   [ ] _____

[ ] _____   [ ] _____

Today I am feeling...

_____

_____

_____

take a moment to release any fear, doubt, or negativity...

Three things I intend to do for myself:
(If reflecting, three things I did for myself)

1._____

2._____

3._____

How will I serve others?
(If reflecting, how did I serve others?)

_____

_____

_____

_____

Three things I am grateful for:

1. _____

2. _____

3. _____

talk about anything...

_____

_____

_____

_____

_____

_____

_____

___ / ___ / ___

Today's Intention:

_____

_____

Affirmation:_____

Major Tasks/Goals:

[ ] _____   [ ] _____

[ ] _____   [ ] _____

[ ] _____   [ ] _____

Today I am feeling...

_____

_____

_____

take a moment to release any fear, doubt, or negativity...

Three things I intend to do for myself:
(If reflecting, three things I did for myself)

1._____

2._____

3._____

How will I serve others?
(If reflecting, how did I serve others?)

_____

_____

_____

_____

Three things I am grateful for:

1. _____

2. _____

3. _____

talk about anything…

_____

_____

_____

_____

_____

_____

_____

___/___/___

Today's Intention:

_____

_____

Affirmation:_____

Major Tasks/Goals:

[ ] _____   [ ] _____

[ ] _____   [ ] _____

[ ] _____   [ ] _____

Today I am feeling…

_____

_____

_____

take a moment to release any fear, doubt, or negativity…

Three things I intend to do for myself:
(If reflecting, three things I did for myself)

1._____

2._____

3._____

How will I serve others?
(If reflecting, how did I serve others?)

_____

_____

_____

_____

Three things I am grateful for:

1. _____

2. _____

3. _____

talk about anything…

_____

_____

_____

_____

_____

_____

_____

___ / ___ / ___

Today's Intention:

_____

_____

Affirmation:_____

Major Tasks/Goals:

[ ] _____   [ ] _____

[ ] _____   [ ] _____

[ ] _____   [ ] _____

Today I am feeling...

_____

_____

_____

take a moment to release any fear, doubt, or negativity...

Three things I intend to do for myself:
(If reflecting, three things I did for myself)

1._____

2._____

3._____

How will I serve others?
(If reflecting, how did I serve others?)

_____

_____

_____

_____

Three things I am grateful for:

1. _____

2. _____

3. _____

talk about anything…

_____

_____

_____

_____

_____

_____

_____

___ / ___ / ___

Today's Intention:

_____

_____

Affirmation:_____

Major Tasks/Goals:

[ ] _____   [ ] _____

[ ] _____   [ ] _____

[ ] _____   [ ] _____

Today I am feeling...

_____

_____

_____

take a moment to release any fear, doubt, or negativity...

Three things I intend to do for myself:
(If reflecting, three things I did for myself)

1._____

2._____

3._____

How will I serve others?
(If reflecting, how did I serve others?)

_____

_____

_____

_____

Three things I am grateful for:

1. _____

2. _____

3. _____

talk about anything...

_____

_____

_____

_____

_____

_____

_____

___/___/___

Today's Intention:

_____

_____

Affirmation:_____

Major Tasks/Goals:

[ ] _____   [ ] _____

[ ] _____   [ ] _____

[ ] _____   [ ] _____

Today I am feeling...

_____

_____

_____

take a moment to release any fear, doubt, or negativity...

Three things I intend to do for myself:
(If reflecting, three things I did for myself)

1._____

2._____

3._____

How will I serve others?
(If reflecting, how did I serve others?)

_____

_____

_____

_____

Three things I am grateful for:

1. _____

2. _____

3. _____

talk about anything...

_____

_____

_____

_____

_____

_____

_____

___/___/___

Today's Intention:

_____

_____

Affirmation:_____

Major Tasks/Goals:

[ ] _____   [ ] _____

[ ] _____   [ ] _____

[ ] _____   [ ] _____

Today I am feeling…

_____

_____

_____

take a moment to release any fear, doubt, or negativity…

Three things I intend to do for myself:
(If reflecting, three things I did for myself)

1._____

2._____

3._____

How will I serve others?
(If reflecting, how did I serve others?)

_____

_____

_____

_____

Three things I am grateful for:

1. _____

2. _____

3. _____

talk about anything...

_____

_____

_____

_____

_____

_____

___/___/___

Today's Intention:

_____

_____

Affirmation:_____

Major Tasks/Goals:

[ ] _____   [ ] _____

[ ] _____   [ ] _____

[ ] _____   [ ] _____

Today I am feeling...

_____

_____

_____

take a moment to release any fear, doubt, or negativity...

Three things I intend to do for myself:
(If reflecting, three things I did for myself)

1._____

2._____

3._____

How will I serve others?
(If reflecting, how did I serve others?)

_____

_____

_____

_____

Three things I am grateful for:

1. _____

2. _____

3. _____

talk about anything...

_____

_____

_____

_____

_____

_____

_____

Watered: a daily journal of intention

___ / ___ / ___

Today's Intention:

_____

_____

Affirmation:_____

Major Tasks/Goals:

[ ] _____   [ ] _____

[ ] _____   [ ] _____

[ ] _____   [ ] _____

Today I am feeling...

_____

_____

_____

take a moment to release any fear, doubt, or negativity...

Three things I intend to do for myself:
(If reflecting, three things I did for myself)

1._____

2._____

3._____

How will I serve others?
(If reflecting, how did I serve others?)

_____

_____

_____

_____

Three things I am grateful for:

1. _____

2. _____

3. _____

talk about anything…

_____

_____

_____

_____

_____

_____

___ / ___ / ___

Today's Intention:

_____

_____

Affirmation:_____

Major Tasks/Goals:

[ ] _____   [ ] _____

[ ] _____   [ ] _____

[ ] _____   [ ] _____

Today I am feeling...

_____

_____

_____

take a moment to release any fear, doubt, or negativity...

Three things I intend to do for myself:
(If reflecting, three things I did for myself)

1._____

2._____

3._____

How will I serve others?
(If reflecting, how did I serve others?)

_____

_____

_____

_____

Three things I am grateful for:

1. _____

2. _____

3. _____

talk about anything…

_____

_____

_____

_____

_____

_____

_____

____ / ___ / ___

Today's Intention:

_____

_____

Affirmation:_____

Major Tasks/Goals:

[ ] _____   [ ] _____

[ ] _____   [ ] _____

[ ] _____   [ ] _____

Today I am feeling…

_____

_____

_____

take a moment to release any fear, doubt, or negativity…

Three things I intend to do for myself:
(If reflecting, three things I did for myself)

1._____

2._____

3._____

How will I serve others?
(If reflecting, how did I serve others?)

_____

_____

_____

_____

Three things I am grateful for:

1. _____

2. _____

3. _____

talk about anything...

_____

_____

_____

_____

_____

_____

___/___/___

Today's Intention:

_____

_____

Affirmation:_____

Major Tasks/Goals:

[ ] _____   [ ] _____

[ ] _____   [ ] _____

[ ] _____   [ ] _____

Today I am feeling...

_____

_____

_____

take a moment to release any fear, doubt, or negativity...

Three things I intend to do for myself:
(If reflecting, three things I did for myself)

1._____

2._____

3._____

How will I serve others?
(If reflecting, how did I serve others?)

_____

_____

_____

_____

Three things I am grateful for:

1. _____

2. _____

3. _____

talk about anything…

_____

_____

_____

_____

_____

_____

___/ ___/ ___

Today's Intention:

_____

_____

Affirmation:_____

Major Tasks/Goals:

[ ] _____   [ ] _____

[ ] _____   [ ] _____

[ ] _____   [ ] _____

Today I am feeling…

_____

_____

_____

take a moment to release any fear, doubt, or negativity…

Three things I intend to do for myself:
(If reflecting, three things I did for myself)

1._____

2._____

3._____

How will I serve others?
(If reflecting, how did I serve others?)

_____

_____

_____

_____

Three things I am grateful for:

1. _____

2. _____

3. _____

talk about anything...

_____

_____

_____

_____

_____

_____

___/ ___/ ___

Today's Intention:

_____

_____

Affirmation:_____

Major Tasks/Goals:

[ ] _____   [ ] _____

[ ] _____   [ ] _____

[ ] _____   [ ] _____

Today I am feeling…

_____

_____

_____

take a moment to release any fear, doubt, or negativity…

Three things I intend to do for myself:
(If reflecting, three things I did for myself)

1._____

2._____

3._____

How will I serve others?
(If reflecting, how did I serve others?)

_____

_____

_____

_____

Three things I am grateful for:

1. _____

2. _____

3. _____

talk about anything...

_____

_____

_____

_____

_____

_____

___/___/___

Today's Intention:

_____

_____

Affirmation:_____

Major Tasks/Goals:

[ ] _____   [ ] _____

[ ] _____   [ ] _____

[ ] _____   [ ] _____

Today I am feeling…

_____

_____

_____

take a moment to release any fear, doubt, or negativity…

Three things I intend to do for myself:
(If reflecting, three things I did for myself)

1._____

2._____

3._____

How will I serve others?
(If reflecting, how did I serve others?)

_____

_____

_____

_____

Three things I am grateful for:

1. _____

2. _____

3. _____

talk about anything...

_____

_____

_____

_____

_____

_____

_____

Watered: a daily journal of intention

___/___/___

Today's Intention:

_____

_____

Affirmation:_____.

Major Tasks/Goals:

[ ] _____   [ ] _____

[ ] _____   [ ] _____

[ ] _____   [ ] _____

Today I am feeling...

_____

_____

_____

take a moment to release any fear, doubt, or negativity...

Three things I intend to do for myself:
(If reflecting, three things I did for myself)

1._____

2._____

3._____

How will I serve others?
(If reflecting, how did I serve others?)

_____

_____

_____

_____

Three things I am grateful for:

1. _____

2. _____

3. _____

talk about anything...

_____

_____

_____

_____

_____

_____

_____

MONTHLY CHECK-IN

This month was ………………………….. ☺   ☹

Did I meet my goals? ………………………   YES!   Still at it!

I feel _____ about next month.

I will celebrate my accomplishments by:

_____

_____

My favorite affirmation from this month is:

_____

_____

A doodle of this month's progress (it does not need to be linear)

notes to self…

_____

_____

_____

_____

_____

_____

_____

_____

_____

_____

_____

_____

_____

_____

_____

_____

Connect further with Ka'ala

Instagram: @alohakaala
Website: www.alohakaala.com

Made in the USA
Columbia, SC
17 October 2021